Haworth and the Brontës

THE
BRONTË PARSONAGE

HAWORTH

Georgian Parsonage containing many relics of the Brontë family including furniture, clothes, manuscripts and drawings.
Small formal garden.

The Museum is adjacent to the Parish Church of St. Michael in Church Street which leads from Main Street.

Opening Hours:

Open Daily 11 a.m.—6 p.m. (11 a.m.—5 p.m. October to March)

Sunday 2 p.m.—6 p.m. (2 p.m.—5 p.m. October to March)

The Gate closes ½ hr. before the stated closing time.

Admission: Adults 40p; Children and OAPs; 20p
Please note admission charges are subject to revision

Telephone: Haworth 42323

CLOSED LAST 3 WEEKS IN DECEMBER

Haworth and the Brontës

A Visitor's Guide
by W. R. Mitchell

JOHN SELBY

Dalesman Books
1981

The Dalesman Publishing Company Ltd.

Clapham, Via Lancaster, LA2 8EB.

First published 1967
Second edition 1969
Third edition 1971
Sixth impression 1981
© W.R. Mitchell 1967, 1981

ISBN: 0 85206 120 X

Printed by Galava Printing Company Limited, Hallam Road, Nelson, Lancashire.

Contents

1. The Story of Haworth 7

2. Introducing the Brontës 12

3. Haunts of the Brontës 25

4. Walks in the Brontë Country 42

5. Places known to the Brontës 53

6. The Novels of the Brontës 56

7. Brontë Personalities 62

8. A Railway came to Haworth 65

Illustrations

The cover photograph, of Top Withens, was provided by T. Pettit, F.R.S.A. The back cover illustration of Anne, Emily and Charlotte Brontë is from a painting by Branwell Brontë, courtesy National Portrait Gallery. Maps and sketches on pages 10, 17, 26, 41, 44-45, 55 by E. Gower.

The Photographs:

W. R. Mitchell—upper picture on 38, 31; National Portrait Gallery—33; G. Bernard Wood—33; Ian Dewhirst collection—right hand subject on page 40; S. Outram—middle picture on 38; Clifford Robinson—36-37; E. W. Tattersall—lower picture on page 37.

The Drawings:

John Selby—title page; Joseph Appleyard—15; William Scruton's "Thornton and the Brontës"—34, 25; Leonard E. Kersley—47; R. B. Evans—upper drawing on 51; D. K. Harris—lower drawing on 51; A. Taylor—59; Betty Whiteoak—61.

Haworth Handloom Weavers

117 Main Street,
Haworth
nr. Keighley

Telephone:
Haworth 42674

SPECIALISTS IN NATURAL FIBRES

All Wool Cloths, Ties and Rugs
Mohair/Wool Scarves, Stoles and Rugs

Stockists for Andrew Stewart Mohair
Garment and co-ordinating Tweeds and
Lambswool Knitwear

1. The Story of Haworth

Speak of the North—a lonely moor
Silent and still and trackless lies.
Charlotte Brontë.

The old stone houses are high compared with the
width of the street, which makes an abrupt turn before
reaching the more level ground at the head of the
village, so that the steep aspect of the place in one
part is almost like that of a wall.
Mrs. Gaskell, Charlotte's biographer,
approaching Haworth from Keighley (1857).

HAWORTH is a hillside village in the West Riding of Yorkshire. It was once a distinct and fiercely independent community, but since 1938 it has been a ward of Keighley. Haworth's feet are in the industrialised Worth Valley; its head rests on moors which rise to well over 1,000 feet above sea level. But for the Brontës it would be no better known than scores of other stone-and-slate villages on the Pennines. The Brontës and their writings, their sombre and rather sad lives close to the moors, have given Haworth an international appeal. There are some 220,000 visitors a year to the Brontë Parsonage Museum alone.

Haworth began with the moors. It was up here, well clear of the unhealthy, impassable marsh and scrubland of the valleys, that man made his first marks on the local landscape. Here were the first small settlements, the first clearings for stock and the first tentative cuts in the ground for crops. The story of Haworth has been the story of a gradual descent of human activity to valley level—from the first crude attempts at farming and weaving on the skyline down to the sophisticated workplaces close to the major streams and rivers but now, through electricity, independent of them.

In its middle years as a village, Haworth heard the clack of handlooms, and there were still 1,200 of them in the days of the Brontës. The spirit of handwork, which was killed by the factories, lived on at Stanbury until 1910. That was the year that Timmy Feather—"last of the handloom weavers"—died, his loom and accessories being later moved to Keighley, first to Victoria Park Museum and eventually to a spacious site in Cliffe Castle.

Along the old tracks, which are now grassed over or were given a durable covering by the road-makers, passed much of the wealth of the West Riding—wool being transported to the markets, or consigned to spinners in the quiet villages of the upper dales and money to pay outstanding dues. The Pennines can still be inhospitable to travellers, and there is still a dark solemnity about the southern moors, including those close to Haworth. The main visible rock is millstone grit. It was so called because millers favoured it highly. It had a coarseness which did not overheat the grain. Large areas of moorland are blanketed by peat, here and there eroded by wind into great, moist slabs which have the rich colour of chocolate cake. The peat formed slowly from the decay of vegetation like the cotton grass which whitens many a moortop as though with summer snow. For those who do not see it on a moorland walk there is a sight of peat and cotton grass from some of the highest roads, such as that linking Haworth and Lancashire through Stanbury or the road from Oxenhope to Hebden Bridge.

The moors support heather, the commonest of which is ling. In summer and autumn its tiny blossoms, viewed collectively, give the impression that a giant has unrolled a purple carpet on the hills. Here, too, is the moorcock—the stubby-winged red grouse—shouting "go back, go back" to intruders in a voice which is close to the range of a human voice. Tufts of nardus grass, known to Pennine farmers as "bent", compete with the heather, with bilberry and other moorland fruits. The most exotic which grows on the highest points of the Haworth moors is cloud-berry, "the mountain strawberry". It produces tasty orange berries at the time of grouse-shooting.

Moorland streams, biting deep into the ground, have created the V-shaped valleys, or cloughs, which have miniature jungles of bracken in them. The tinkle of water is heard everywhere and especially at what are now known as the Brontë Falls, where two streams meet and send water into Lower Laithe Reservoir. Ponden Reservoir has taken some of the spirit from the nursery reaches of the Worth on which Keighley was founded. Leeshaw Reservoir is seen by motorists near Oxenhope.

Crossing part of the Haworth Moors is the Pennine Way, Britain's longest continuous footpath. It is 250 miles long and cannot be trudged in its entirety in less than a fortnight by those who are not out to break records. The Pennine Way starts at Edale in Derbyshire; in the Haworth district it runs close to Ponden Reservoir. Features on the Haworth Moors seem isolated but are not very far from metalled roads. Even Top Withens, which is held up as the ultimate in isolation—and is the proto-type, some think, of Emily Brontë's Wuthering Heights—is little more than a mile from the road which passes Ponden Hall. The approach to it is normally from near Stanbury, and then the distance is greater. Straight lines are best left to the crows because of the undulations of the countryside.

Stanbury, about which Halliwell Sutcliffe wrote extensively —*The Man of the Moors* and *Ricroft of Withens*, for example— has kept the flavour of a moorland village, being at a slightly higher level than Haworth and straggling alongside the road from Haworth by Trawden Forest to Colne. Because the devel-opment of Haworth was downhill, towards the big concentra-tions of houses and industries around the Bridgehouse Beck and in the lower Worth Valley, the area around the church and par-sonage remains close to open country. Stand near the parsonage and you hear lark song and the exuberant display calls of the lapwing. Industrialisation close to this part of Haworth took the form of stone quarrying, which made the countryside even more rugged.

Haworth's earliest written history was concerned with the church. The village name first appears in Kirkby's Inquest, 1296. Incumbents of Haworth lived at Sowdens from 1739. We have certain records of the church in transcript form at York from 1600, but in Haworth only from 1645 when the parish registers commenced. In those registers were noted the interments of the area. Over 40,000 burials took place in the graveyard which the Brontës saw from the front windows of their parsonage home. With a new surge of interest in education about the time of Queen Elizabeth I the village of Haworth acquired a grammar school. The Civil Wars left marks on its life, notably in 1654, when its incumbent, the Rev. John Collier, was expelled because he was a Royalist.

During the 18th century came the divines: William Grimshaw, John and Charles Wesley. Grimshaw was the perpetual curate at Haworth for 21 years from 1742 and he made the place very much his own. He arrived at a Haworth which shared with so many villages in England at that time a very poor view of clergy-men. The voice of the Anglican church was a faint whisper. Grimshaw, a man of intense fervour, which led him into a close friendship with John Wesley and the Methodists, would start his services with a long hymn which enabled him to grab a whip, leap over the wall around the church and scour the inns for reluctant worshippers who sometimes felt the sting of the whip

9

about them as they were driven to church.

He was a man who did not mince words. His rough, relentless manner was one way of command-ing attention from a religiously-slack commun-ity; he was also a man of great humility who was constantly searching his soul; he had a selfless regard for his flock, par-ticularly those who were in ill health. William Grim-shaw met the Wesleys in 1746, and at his invitation

Haworth Parsonage before extensions.

they preached at Haworth church. He admired the work of itinerant Methodist preachers, and made his own rounds of the Haworth district to take services in cottages. When John Wesley preached at Haworth in August, 1748, the service began at 5 a.m. and he later spoke to 4,000 people who had assembled in the graveyard. Grimshaw then walked with Wesley the nine miles to Colne, and here another service was held. It was Grimshaw who made Haworth church a more imposing building in 1755.

Oliver Heywood's independent ministry was earlier than Grimshaw's. He was one of the ministers ejected from the church because he refused to conform to the prayer-book in its entirety. He found friends among the farmfolk of West Craven, and from here his ministry spread about the Pennines. He kept careful note of what he saw, and wrote graphically about a hot dry summer of 1681 when "people began to despair of rain". Heywood "saw the dreadfullest sights of bare pastures in my travels that my eyes saw scarce any green thing left in fields. I saw both in Haworth parish and on towards Marsden the strangest fires upon the moores that have been known, burning up the heath and dry mossy earth many miles forward and could not be quenched."

The Haworth of the 17th century had its wild moments, as on "Lords day July 12, 1680". Then there was a rushbearing at Haworth "and the Tyde revelling (as they call it) on which multi-tudes of people meet, feast, drink, play and commit many outrages in rantings, riding, without any fear of restraint—"the munday which is the day after they call Crowmoors (Crow Moor)? day, then they make races and continue in drinkings, vanitys, it may be longer: oh dreadful!"

Haworth in Heywood's time had its mysteries, for in the January of 1664 (as the zestful evangelist noted) "was a trumpet heard in the aire about Haworth and Stanbury by several familys that were called out to hear the sound; it terrified a caryers horses; it sound long and went on as if it went towards Lanc; it seemed musical, and sounded like an Howboy as they say that heard it."

What did Heywood think of Haworth when he first visited it? He called it "a very ignorant place, where there was never good preaching, multitudes of people flockt to hear me, some were affected, god helped my heart graciously in praying and preaching about four hours together; it was strange preaching amongst them; who knows what work god may haue on some hearts?" His great friend locally was Jonas Foster, and services were usually held at Foster's home.

It was Heywood, then, who made the first deep cuts into Haworth religious apathy, and Grimshaw and the Wesleys (but notably Grimshaw) deepened and rationalised the work of conversion which saw the enlargement of the church and the building of Nonconformist chapels, with the Baptists opening a place of worship in 1752 and the Methodists acting six years later. The parsonage which was to be the home of the Brontës was built in 1779.

The Brontë association lasted for 41 years, from the coming of the family in 1820 until the death of the old parson, Patrick in 1861. Since then Haworth's life and development have been largely conditioned by the veneration shown to the family. Much of the exterior of the parsonage is as they would recall, except a wing was added in 1872. Extensions were made in the rear by the Brontë Society, who acquired the property by the generosity of Sir James Roberts in 1928. The church is quite different from that in which Patrick Brontë preached. Haworth threw off its subservience to Bradford in 1864 and became a distinct parish. Most of the old church was pulled down in 1879; a new church was being used in 1881. The stone setts in the steep main street remain, and so do many of the houses known to the Brontës. Railway station, mills, terraced housing and later the bus terminus were established much lower down the hill than the area of the church. Today, visitors walking up from the railway station (which is now a railway museum) who wish to avoid congestion on the narrow main street pass through a pleasant park.

They reach an area which Brontë interest has frozen in its Victorian stage of development. It is not the whole Haworth, for progressive forces were at work lower down the hill, but it is the area for tourists. Here the Brontë story can seem very recent indeed.

2. Introducing the Brontës

The story of the Brontë sisters is the most romantic
in the history of literature, full of comedy and pathos,
yet bearing witness to the indomitable spirit that
dwelt within these weakly consumptive girls.

Prof. C. E. M. Joad (1924).

There is something very compelling in the thought of
these girls, the daughters of a clergyman whose parish
lay on the edge of the moors, writing masterpieces by
firelight, while the wind whistled round the corners of
the house, and their brother was drinking in "The
Black Bull" down the street. Our literature can have
few stranger scenes than this.

Norman Swallow, introducing a radio
programme (1949).

THE Brontë family arrived in Haworth on an April day in
1820. Seven farm carts were used to move their belongings
from Thornton, where the Rev. Patrick Brontë had ministered
for five years. The women and children travelled in a light wagon
which was covered in to cheat the Pennine breezes. The carrier
said to one of his friends that the Brontë children were so small
he "could have put them all under a clothes basket".

Patrick Brontë was a "well-built, good-looking man" (in the
recollection of Abraham Holroyd, who lived at Clayton). His
tall figure had a slight stoop to it. Around his chin was the
smallest of beards which could be kept in good shape by a
four-times-a-year clipping. Maria, his Cornish wife, made the
journey with some foreboding, for though she was capable and
well-educated, her health was poor, and coming to Yorkshire
from one of the sunniest counties in England she had never
quite adapted herself to its chilling dampness. Maria Branwell

had met the clergyman who was her husband when holiday-making with relatives at Woodhouse School, Apperley Bridge. He was the curate of Hartshead at the time. The marriage had taken place at Guiseley eight years before they moved to Haworth. In those eight years she had given birth to six children —to Maria and Elizabeth (born at Hartshead); Charlotte, Patrick Branwell, Emily Jane and Anne (born in the double-fronted house in Thornton's main street). Anne then was only about four months old.

Patrick Brontë's appointment was to the "perpetual curacy" of Haworth. The church here was a chapel-of-ease to Bradford, and a curate could hold the appointment for life. Brontë succeeded the Rev. James Charnock, who died in May 1819, if you except a very brief stay by the Rev. S. Redhead. The Vicar of Bradford appointed the Haworth incumbent, but local support was necessary. Local hands gripped the purse into which land rents were placed and from which most of the stipend was paid. The people objected to Brontë not because they were opposed to him as a man but because there was no love for the vicar. Patrick wisely demurred. His grace and courtesy on this occasion stood him in good stead later on. Mr. Redhead, who had ministered here during the illness of Mr. Charnock, was the next choice. He was bolder, going against local wishes. He paid the penalty for his daring.

Mr. Redhead's ministry lasted for three weeks, and then he retired, his spirit crushed. On the first Sunday he preached to a full church, but the worshippers left noisily, their clogs clattering on the flagstones, until parson and clerk had the church to themselves. On the following Sunday a man rode an ass down the church. He was sitting facing the wrong way, and his head was festooned with old hats. In the uproar which followed his appearance the curate left the building.

Maybe Mr. Redhead thought he could break the spirit of the Haworthians; he put on a brave front next Sunday by riding up the main street with some Bradford gentlemen, hoping perhaps to impress the people. They were irritated, and supplied a chimney sweep with much strong drink; they took the sweep to church and reared him before the reading desk. With blackened face he nodded a stupid assent to all that the hapless curate said. The sweep climbed into the pulpit and tried to embrace Mr. Redhead, who fled to the *Black Bull* and managed to escape the wrath of the people, leaving through a little-frequented door. The Vicar of Bradford resigned. Mr. Brontë was invited to take over at Haworth.

Patrick Brontë had been born a Prunty, or Brunty, at Emdale near Loughbrickland, in county Down. His birthplace was a rough log cabin. Father was an illiterate peasant who had 10 children. The start was unpromising, but Patrick was lucky to be befriended by a Protestant clergyman who helped him with his education. In 1802, when he was 25 years of age, Patrick Brontë was at Cambridge, and he graduated in 1806 with a B.A. By now his family name had become Brontë because of his admiration for Lord Nelson, who was created Duke of Brontë in 1799. The young Irishman was also using the diaeresis which has become a nuisance to writers about the Brontës ever since!

His vocation as a clergyman began with a curacy in Essex. He came to the West Riding of Yorkshire, first to Dewsbury, then to Hartshead-cum-Clifton. It was a time of massive and at times violent social changes as the old cottage industries of the Pennine area declined and the factory system was developed. The industrial revolution, the change from widespread rural handwork to concentrated effort in towns, was attended by poverty and misery among many working class families. It was a time when Luddites met to plot machine-smashing expeditions. The pugnacious spirit between masters and their men had an echo in the relationships which existed between the clergy and the ministers of Nonconformity. There was a revolution in religious ideas as well.

Patrick Brontë went about his ministry and when there was spare time he wrote verse. He set down his impressions of cabin life in Ireland; he recalled the beauties of the Mourne Mountains. This clergyman with a scholarly bent turned out very ordinary verse, but in 1811, when he was at Hartshead, his first little book of poems was published.

He had a great friend in the clergy. The Rev. William Morgan was curate at Bradford, and Morgan was engaged to be married to the daughter of Mr. John Fennell, master of Woodhouse Grove School. Patrick Brontë had his minor infatuations, and at times he had contemplated marriage. Morgan introduced him to the Fennells, and it was at their home that he met Miss Maria Branwell, who was about 28 years of age and on holiday in Yorkshire from her home at Penzance. They were attached to each other. So rapid was the courtship that a twin ceremony was arranged, at which Mr. Morgan officiated at Brontë's wedding and then Patrick Brontë officiated at the wedding of Mr. Morgan. The Brontë children arrived with great regularity, and each confinement further weakened the frail Maria Brontë. In the April of 1820, when the family arrived at Haworth, she had only 17 months to live.

They came to a village which, while on the moor edge, was by no means at the back o' beyond socially. A well-used route from the West Riding into Lancashire passed through Haworth and Stanbury. The villagers were a lively lot, and the oldest of them could remember Grimshaw's stirring ministry, for he died less than sixty years before. If there was an octogenarian in the

Haworth of 1820 that person might have recalled the visit of John Wesley, when not only was the church packed but thousands of people stood in the graveyard to hear him preach. It is unlikely that the Haworth people loved Brontë during his years of ministry (it was not easy to love such an austere man) but they undoubtedly grew to respect him.

The Haworth parsonage to which his family and possessions were taken was a rather pleasant house built of Yorkshire sandstone with generous Georgian proportions. It faced east, towards the church, with a view of the enormous graveyard, where tombstones are reared in long rows like battalions of stone men. Still, the parsonage was larger than the parson's house had been at

Thornton. It was palatial compared with Patrick Brontë's original Irish home. None of the rooms was vast, but they had pleasant proportions. There was a water pump in the kitchen.

Behind the parsonage lay open country (it is still very open), where small farms were laced together by dry-stone walls. It was a type of countryside Patrick Brontë had grown to know during his five years at Thornton. He would visit farms on the hills and already had become familiar with the becking of the red grouse, the reedy but exuberant mating cries of the lapwings, and the minstrelsy of the curlews in spring. The family growing up at Haworth (growing in a village where the average expectancy of life was 27 years) found, not very far from the darkly-clustering houses of the village, a big, open, colourful, at times savage wilderness, where the wind could blow so fiercely

that Ruskin would later write: "One may lean against a Yorkshire breeze as one would against a quickset hedge."

Patrick Brontë attended to his parish duties, and helped to raise support for measures against local lawlessness brought about by unsettled social conditions. He loaded up two pistols each evening in case of intrusion during the night, and he gravely discharged the pistols from an upper window each morning. In the absence of a mother, the children were looked after by Miss Branwell, an aunt who, according to Ellen Nussey, a later friend of Charlotte, was "a small antiquated little lady". In their growing-up they also grew to love Tabitha Aykroyd, who came into Brontë service in 1825, and Martha Brown. Martha arrived in the household in 1840 and was a faithful servant right through to the time of Patrick Brontë's death, the last in his family, in 1861.

The children, and particularly Emily, were to find on the moors much of the inspiration their imaginative Celtic minds needed. They must express themselves, and as much of their time was spent indoors this expression largely took the form of a fantasy world whose doings were recorded in tiny books. Overall was the void left by the passing of Maria Brontë, their mother. When she died of cancer in September, 1821, she was aged 38 years.

Life at the parsonage, then, was self-contained. The Brontë children were not encouraged to mix with children from the village (if, indeed, the village youth would have felt at ease with the young folk from the curate's house). Miss Branwell taught them needlework. Father told them stories of the old days, which further fired their imagination, and

Hightown, Thornton.

he also developed in them a thirst for knowledge.

The Rev. W. Carus-Wilson, Rector of Tunstall, had started a school for daughters of the clergy. It stood beside the Keighley-Kendal turnpike road at Cowan Bridge. The Brontë girls were enrolled, Maria and Elizabeth arriving in July, 1824. Their experiences were not very happy, and later their misery was reflected in print and Cowan Bridge School became the "Lowood" of Charlotte's *Jane Eyre*. This unhappiness was not

17

entirely the fault of the Rev. Carus-Wilson. The Brontë girls were not robust. They had their schooling through a bleak winter. They had not been away from home before and were homesick. Apart from the lessons, there were exacting weekly journeys to Tunstall Church, which lay two-and-a-half miles away through the fields. A cold lunch was served to them in a little room over the porch.

In the spring of 1825, when they might have responded to improved climatic conditions, an outbreak of low fever occurred. Maria was sent home to Haworth on February 14th. She died of tuberculosis on May 6th. Elizabeth followed her home on May 31st, and she died of the same complaint. Tuberculosis, known more widely as "consumption", was one of the killer diseases of the time.

For six years the Haworth parsonage held all the remaining Brontës. Then Charlotte went away to school once again, this time to Roe Head, a private school run by the Misses Wooler. Roe Head not only completed her formal education but it introduced this strangely withdrawn young woman to two others who were to become friends for life. They were Ellen Nussey and Mary Taylor. In later years Charlotte wrote to them frequently; from the letters that have been preserved we have information about the day-to-day life of the Brontës which richly augments the sparse information to be gathered elsewhere. When Charlotte left Roe Head she was 16 years of age.

The pride and joy of the Brontës was Patrick Branwell, the only son. He early showed artistic qualities, and so it was the ambition of the family that he should become a great artist. An art teacher came from Leeds to instruct him, and Branwell later set himself up as a portrait painter in Bradford, a career which did not last very long. In 1839 he was at Broughton, north-west of Morecambe Bay, working as a tutor at Mr. Postlethwaite's school.

Charlotte returned to Misses Wooler's school as a teacher in 1835. Emily accompanied her, but Emily was dreadfully homesick and she fretted for Haworth, returning home after only three months. Anne Brontë took Emily's place at Roe Head in 1836. It was a time of comings and goings at the parsonage. Charlotte returned from Roe Head. Emily left home to become a teacher at Law Hill, Southowram, Halifax, in the autumn of 1837 under Miss Patchett, a job which lasted only six months. The work was hard, spread over 18 hours a day, but homesickness was strong and compulsive.

Charlotte, now aged 23, became the governess at Stone Gappe, Lothersdale, but she was not very happy. She returned to Haworth and then went off again, to become governess at Upperwood House, Rawdon. Anne became a governess at Blake Hall;

she had less of the restless disposition of her sisters, but the work was hard and Anne was not very strong. She found happier duties at Thorp Green, near York, where she cared for the children of an invalid clergyman.

The jobs available for young women at that time were limited. Teaching was one of the most comely occupations. The Brontë sisters had not been great successes when employed by others, and now they developed a strong desire for running their own school. The project was discussed at length in 1840. To succeed they would have to be more proficient at languages, particularly French, so in 1842, with Miss Branwell's help, Charlotte and Emily went to the Continent to complete their education. They had an introduction to Mme. Heger, who ran a school in Brussels.

Miss Branwell died in October, 1842, and the sisters returned to Haworth. Emily stayed but Charlotte returned to Brussels, as a student teacher in 1843 for £16 per annum. She was prompted "by an irresistible impulse", and fell under the influence of M. Heger. She was, in fact, deeply in love with him, which caused embarrassment, particularly in her relationship with his wife. It was a highly emotional time in Charlotte's life, and but for M. Heger we should not have had *The Professor* and *Villette*. Both these novels give us realistic pictures of the Belgian professor, with his heavy black moustache and black hair, and of Mme. Heger, forever peeping behind doors and listening in the corridors leading to the schoolrooms for anything that should offend her capricious taste. It is tantalising to imagine what the professor really thought about Charlotte, apart from the vanity any man would have in the touching show of love and craving for understanding showed by this young woman from a Yorkshire parsonage. Charlotte was not one of the best-looking of women. She was small in figure ("stunted" was a word she often used herself), and her plainness forever worried her.

A worry at this time at Haworth parsonage was the decline of Branwell Brontë. Branwell had been in railway service as a clerk at Sowerby Bridge and Luddendenfoot, but he neglected his duties and was dismissed from a Thorp Green appointment in 1845 because of his infatuation for the wife of his employer who so promptly after her husband's death married a baronet. In that year of 1845 he felt the whiplash of disgrace and, consequently, the scorn of his own family. Charlotte lost patience with him; she had forgotten her sad experience with the Hegers.

Branwell had the disability of his mother and his sisters. He suffered from tuberculosis, and as the disease advanced his constitution was badly affected. He took laudanum to ease the pain. Mental release he found in the less formal atmosphere of the *Black Bull Inn*, at the top of Haworth's main street, where he always had a ready audience because he was by nature a charmer and a skilled user of words in conversation.

The years 1845 to 1848 were haunted by drink and opium, debts and delusion, and only one man close to the Brontës remained faithful to him throughout this unhappy period. This was John Brown, the sexton, father of Martha Brown, servant at the parsonage. Branwell remained vigorous even at the end. He was ill in bed for a day; then, on a Sunday morning, he struggled to his feet and died standing up. The death certificate gave the death as "chronic bronchitis, marasmus". Branwell was 31 years of age.

It was not the only sorrow to hit the family. Patrick Brontë was in poor health. He suffered blindness, and Charlotte accompanied him to Manchester in 1846 where a successful operation was performed. Against this background—against the accumulating sadness—were penned some of the most memorable lines in English literature. The success in writing was to come not to Patrick Brontë, whose aspirations with a pen were great, nor to Branwell who, in other circumstances, would also have been capable of literary greatness. It came to the Brontë sisters—to Charlotte, Emily and Anne—who for years had poured out their souls in a stream of literary make-belief. They passed many a Haworth afternoon in fanciful worlds, like the Gondal of Emily and Anne or the Angria of Charlotte and Branwell; the affairs were chronicled in tiny notebooks. The sisters, drawn together by tragedy, discovered a mutual interest in verse when Charlotte found some of Emily's poems (much to Emily's embarrassment) and persuaded her to have them included in a slim volume which they published at their own expense. For that book they chose pen-names, retaining their own initials—Currer, Ellis and Acton Bell.

It is only in recent times that verse written by the Brontës has been properly assessed. Emily's work has been brought to a prominence which for years was given to Charlotte. The reputation of the Brontë sisters was established through their novels. Emily's tale was the strangely-moving *Wuthering Heights.* Charlotte drew on her experiences in Brussels for *The Professor.* Anne wrote *Agnes Grey.* They used the pen-names which had adorned the verse they published earlier.

The novels of Emily and Anne were accepted, but publication was sadly delayed. Charlotte had no success in placing *The Professor* (it was not published until after her death), but a publisher said he would consider a longer novel. The writing of *Jane Eyre* was begun in Manchester at the time of Patrick Brontë's eye operation. It was published two months before the works of Emily and Anne, *Wuthering Heights* and *Agnes Grey,* appeared. Generously reviewed, and having big sales in America as well as in Britain, the novel was successful beyond the dreams

of the plain little woman of Haworth. *Jane Eyre's* enduring success rests on its literary qualities, but one of the aspects of its publication which stimulated sales was a measure of adverse criticism it received. For this book, with its plain heroine (plain like its author), was a novel such as the world had never seen before. It was unconventional. There was a frankness about its views on life as illustrated by its characters which jolted the rather prim circles in which novels circulated at that time. Thackeray was one man who admired it, and a second edition, in January, 1848, was dedicated to him.

The publication of the Brontë sisters' works was attended by much confusion. All were believed to be the products of one pen. A consideration of the books was often blunted by a discussion on the authorship until, eventually, this was made known. Then the works could be considered unhindered by speculation. Haworth became nationally renowned.

A year after the publication of *Wuthering Heights*, possibly the most powerful of all the Brontë works and, for all its constructional faults, one of the really big events in the story of English literature, its author, Emily, was dead, and until almost the end she refused medical aid. She was 30 years of age. A few months later, while on a visit to Scarborough, Anne died and was buried in St. Mary's churchyard. She was the only member of the family to be buried outside Haworth. There remained in the parsonage the elderly Patrick Brontë and Charlotte, who continued to write. Into *Shirley* she crystallised her feelings for her sister Emily, for this novel is believed to have as its central character the Emily that might have been had she lived under different circumstances. Her setting was the Calder Valley.

Charlotte meanwhile kept up her correspondence with Ellen Nussey, and occasionally she referred to marriage. "The man I marry," she confined, "must be able to inspire an attachment so intense that I would willingly die for him; and if ever I do marry, it must be in the light of that adoration that I will regard my husband. If he were a clever man and loved me, the whole world weighed in the balance against his smallest wish should be as light as air."

Charlotte thought of love as an exalted passion; it was the love she wrote about in her books. She had her chances, but she turned them down. There was the Rev. Henry Nussey, brother of her great friend. "I scorn deceit," she wrote to him, "and I will never for the sake of attaining the distinction of matrimony, and escaping the stings of an old maid, take a worthy man whom I am convinced I could not render happy."

As the years went by, Charlotte's great love did not appear, and the episode involving M. Heger in Brussels, though never entirely forgotten (as two of her novels show), cooled a little. "I am certainly doomed to be an old maid," she wrote with mock resignation. "Never mind. I made up my mind to that fate ever since I was twelve years old." The years of loneliness and sorrow passed, brightened by the success of her literary efforts. There were other suitors. Mr. Taylor, a partner in her publishing firm, left England for five years to recover from the grief of his failure to impress her.

The Rev. A. B. Nicholls came to Haworth in 1844 to assist Mr. Brontë. The good-looking young Irishman had ten years to wait for Charlotte's assent, but he showed great patience. She was at first not very impressed by him. "I cannot for my life" (she wrote to Ellen Nussey, who had met and formed a good opinion of Mr. Nicholls) "see those interesting germs of goodness you discovered in him; his narrowness of mind always strikes me forcibly. I hear he is indebted to your imagination for his hidden treasure."

Eight years after he first met Charlotte Brontë he could keep his feelings to himself no longer. He was leaving the parsonage after seeing Mr. Brontë one evening when (as Charlotte recalled) "he stopped at the door of the room in which I was sitting. He entered: he stood before me. What his words were, you can guess; his manner you can hardly realise, nor can I forget it." Mr. Nicholls was shaking from head to foot, looking very pale, "speaking low, vehemently, yet with difficulty." When father was told of the approach, he stormed and raved and swore. The epithets he heaped on the curate were so vile that Charlotte, though she had no love for the young man, protested. To be fair to Mr. Brontë, he must have been upset that his sole surviving child, and now a national literary figure, should be approached by a curate without substantial means. Mr. Nicholls took the insults badly and, being unable to bear her near presence without hope, he left Haworth. Charlotte could not bring herself to love him despite her sympathy for the way he had been rejected by her father.

Eventually, the storm died down, and Mr. Brontë invited him back to his Haworth curacy. Charlotte, in a neatly devised letter to Ellen Nussey, wrote: "Certainly I must respect him, nor can I withhold him more than mere cold respect. In fact, dear Ellen, I am engaged." They were married in 1854. Charlotte conceived, but the child was not born. The Brontës' physical weakness showed in the last surviving child. On a March morning in 1855 she awoke briefly from a long stupor to find her husband bending over her. He was praying for her life. "Oh! I am not going to die, am I? He will not separate us—we have been so happy," were her last words. On the black-edged mourning card were printed the words: "In Memory of Charlotte Nicholls." A hundred years later, at a special service in Haworth Church, a speaker observed: "We love her because there lies behind those books a human story—a story of triumph and victory over constant adversity."

Mr. Nicholls and Martha Brown remained with the old vicar at the parsonage until he died in June, 1861; Patrick Brontë was 84 years old.

Haunts of the Brontës

In the autumn, the Council consulted our honorary Architect, Mr. Eden, because they were concerned as to the safety of the building, under the constant strain and stress of many feet. Mr. Eden advised that the floor in Mr. Brontë's bedroom should be reinforced with steel girders; and accordingly this work was carried out during Christmas week.

> from the 1966 report of the former Custodian of the Brontë Museum, Joanna Hutton.

Certain classes of people tended to come on certain days. Monday was the day when many clergymen visited the parsonage. Thursday was popular with actors.

> Harold G. Mitchell, a former Custodian.

IT would be too much to expect that the places known to the Brontës were unchanged in more than a century but, apart from the inevitable church restorations, changes have been remarkably few.

HARTSHEAD, between Brighouse and Cleckheaton, where the Rev. Patrick Brontë set up home with Maria Branwell following their marriage at Guiseley, and where their two eldest children, Maria and Elizabeth, were born:

Patrick Brontë, the tall, earnest young Irishman, was a bachelor when he reached Hartshead in 1811. His appointment was as curate, and for a time he lodged with farmfolk at Thorn Bush, finding the time to jot down *Cottage Poems*, his first published work, and to take on the job of school inspector. It was as inspector that he received a special welcome at Woodhouse Grove School. Here he met Maria Branwell, who was on holiday from Cornwall. Patrick Brontë proposed to her during an outing they made to Kirkstall Abbey, the former Cistercian house beside the Aire at the edge of Leeds. The courtship was brief, and the couple set up home at the top of Clough Lane, Hightown, where the three-storeyed building that was the parsonage still stands.

At the parish of Hartshead-cum-Clifton the curate found a thriving Anglican cause. His predecessor was the Rev. Hammond Robertson, who had put fresh heart into the parishioners at a time when Nonconformity was spreading quickly in the West Riding. Patrick Brontë continued the Sunday School which Robertson founded (it was possibly the first Sunday School in the North), and he also faced the problems of lawlessness by unemployed textile workers at a time when machines were being installed in new, valley-sited factories. These workers included some fanatics who called themselves Luddites. Solemn pledges were taken that the machines would be destroyed, and there was a particularly violent attack on the Liversedge mill of William Cartwright in which two men died. Patrick Brontë would later tell his daughter Charlotte about the disturbances: a secret meeting of the Luddites at the *Shears Inn*, Liversedge, the gathering of the discontented outside Roe Head School at Mirfield, and their march on the Cartwright mill. Charlotte remembered the stories and the special fervency of the time, for they were woven into her novel *Shirley*. The "Nunnely" of that tale is Hartshead, and the prototype of Charlotte's character Robert Moore was mill-owner Cartwright.

Above: St. Peter's Church, Hartshead.

Left: Thorn Bush Farm, Hightown.

St. Peter's Church, 500 feet above sea level, has altered radically since the Brontës' time. When the building was restored in 1881 the architect took his cue from two Norman arches. Dormer windows were installed in the roof. Patrick Brontë's portrait is the second in a collection displayed in the vestry. There is also a portrait of 1809 showing him as a serious-looking young man with prominent "sideboards" but no sign of a beard. The setting of the church is largely pastoral, for on one side are green acres of Kirklees Park, where a medieval abbey stood and a mound is pointed out as the burial place of the notable Yorkshire outlaw, Robin Hood, many of whose exploits took place in south-west Yorkshire.

Hartshead reminded Brontë of his marriage to Maria on a December day, 1812; of the birth of the first two of the six children; of the baptism at Hartshead church of the eldest of them, who was named Maria after her mother. Elizabeth, the second child, was baptised at Thornton, and it is very likely that some of the Hartshead parishioners were witnesses of the baptism. For in the early Thornton days he often welcomed his old friends to the services. They had walked from Hartshead to meet him again.

THORNTON, now part of Bradford, where Patrick Brontë was curate for five years and where four of his children were born:

What was a double-fronted parsonage in Brontë days is now 74, Market Street and a private house, with part of the building partitioned off and extended forward to provide a shop and workrooms for a butcher. What was a small, fiercely independent hillside village in Brontë's time is now a big village almost connected physically to Bradford, of which it now forms a part administratively.

That section of the parsonage which remains a home is a fairly big home still, with three bedrooms, a bathroom, kitchen, living room and sitting room. A few steps lead upwards from the butcher's shop into a room where meat products are handled, and this was the birthroom of Charlotte. A distinguishable feature that remains is a fireplace, bricked-up now but retaining the wrought ironwork on which two cherubim are featured.

Patrick Brontë arrived at Thornton in 1815. Details of the Thornton parsonage as it was at the time appear in William Scruton's *Thornton and the Brontës* (published in 1898). Over the door, on a stone slab, are the letters J.A.S. and the date 1802. Scruton tells us that these are the initials of John and Sarah Ashworth, former residents of the village. The hall door in Mr. Brontë's time was reached by several steps. There was a dining room on one side of the hall and a drawing room on the other.

Over the passage to the front was a dressing-room, at the window of which the neighbours often saw Mr. Brontë at his toilet. One of the Thornton Dissenters (there were many Dissenters, who attended services at Kipping Chapel) reported that he had seen the curate shaving himself on a Sunday morning. It was a gross breach of the sabbath as then understood. This was reported to Mr. Brontë, who said: "I should like you to keep what I say in your family, but I never shaved in all my life, or was ever shaved by anyone else. I have so little beard that a little clipping every three months is all that is necessary."

Maria Brontë had her next four children in swift succession. Charlotte was born on April 21st, 1816, followed by her only brother, Branwell (June 26, 1817) and her sisters Emily (July 30, 1818, baptised Emily Jane) and Anne (January 17, 1820). A plaque on the wall of 74, Market Street, Thornton, lists the children who were born within.

The present Anglican church at Thornton, St. James's, stands close to the main road and was consecrated in 1872. The church known to the Brontës also dedicated to St. James, was better known as the Bell Chapel. The parent church was St. Peter's, Bradford. Bell Chapel's story began about 1612 and as the years went by many alterations took place. Patrick Brontë had the church re-roofed, and he also organised the re-fronting of the south side. In his time an imposing cupola was added to the tower.

Pictures showing Bell Chapel in its prime adorn the walls of the vestry at the present church. Just across the road is what remains of the Chapel itself—frames of the east window, with some of the surrounding masonry, and the cupola that was hoisted atop the tower in Brontë's day which now lies, complete, on the ground. All are standing in deep grass, weeds and brambles.

HAWORTH, where Mr. Brontë was curate from February, 1820, until his death, aged 84 years, on June 7th, 1861. Here his wife and all but one of the six children died and were buried. Haworth is the main Brontë centre, and the second most popular place for literary pilgrimage in Britain. First place is occupied by Stratford-on-Avon:

Patrick Brontë was reasonably contented when he settled at Haworth. He wrote: "My salary is not large; it is only about £200 a year. I have a good house, which is mine for life also, and is rent free. No-one has anything to do with the church but myself, and I have a large congregation." The main Brontë sights lie in a compact area around the top of the main street. The present church is post-Brontë, consecrated in 1881. Its graveyard was closed many years ago but was still being used during Patrick

Brontë's curacy. Large trees which give it character now (and which bring to Haworth a colony of rooks whose cawing is among the most English of sounds) were not planted until 1864. The parsonage remains, and since 1928 it has been the main Brontë attraction, being excellently maintained (its rooms adorned with Brontëana) by the Brontë Society.

Close by is the old school where Charlotte taught on Sundays. It was built in 1838, so the Brontë family would see the masons and joiners at work. A close neighbour of the church, as in most communities, is the inn. At Haworth this is the famous *Black Bull*, often visited by Branwell Brontë.

The Parish Church (St. Michael and All Angels): Brontë lovers objected strongly when Mr. Wade, the successor to the Rev. Patrick Brontë, persisted in a proposal to have the old church pulled down and a fresh church built on the site. Only the tower of the old building would be spared. It is tempting to condemn Mr. Wade and to see in his plans a desire to efface something of the Brontë image. Most certainly the growth of the Brontë cult in the latter stages of Patrick Brontë's life and afterwards would weary Mr. Wade and blunt his own ministry. There would be too much harking back to the Brontë days.

In fact, the period when Mr. Wade occupied the parsonage was a more formative time for Haworth than the years of Brontë tenancy. A church which had simply been a chapel-of-ease to Bradford Parish Church, and its incumbent a curate, became a parish in its own right in 1864. The parson was henceforth a rector. Demolishing the old Haworth church was undoubtedly a minor tragedy for those interested in the Brontës (and for lovers of 18th century architecture) but the church which rose in its place was larger and more attractive as the spiritual centre of the parish.

What of the church known to the Brontës? It was a barnlike structure with deep but small-paned windows, looking outwardly as plain as one of the new mills of the valley. Inside were tall wooden pews and galleries. Mr. Brontë had conducted his service from the second deck of the three-decker pulpit, climbing up a storey for the preaching of the sermon. The bottom deck was usually occupied by the parish clerk. This is the church which had served the Rev. William Grimshaw in his prime, and when his ministry resulted in a great increase in the number of worshippers he solved the seating problem, directly and with a minimum of disturbance, by having the church enlarged "two bays eastwards". The three-decker pulpit served Grimshaw and, occasionally, his friends the Wesleys.

Patrick Brontë reached Haworth with a fine record of church renovation. He did not make any notable mark on the fabric of Haworth Church as he had done at Bell Chapel, Thornton. When Mr. Wade had a wholesale clearance of the site except for the tower (which was heightened), he evicted the font used by Grimshaw and Brontë and even the three-decker was dismantled. The top portion is now to be seen in the church at Stanbury. The Brontë spirit has quietly returned to St. Michael's Church through the efforts of those who admired the family. Parson Wade is chiefly remembered for the way he swept away some Brontë connections!

A great admirer of the Brontës, Sir Tresham Lever, Bt., made a handsome gift through which a Brontë Memorial Chapel was created—a chapel dedicated by the Bishop of Bradford in July, 1964, furnished with objects that the Brontës would have known, including a communion table from the old Haworth Church. An American admirer of the life of Charlotte Brontë paid for a stained glass window on which she is commemorated. The Brontë vault is marked by a memorial tablet.

Thornton's registers contain the baptismal details of the three best-known Brontë sisters—Charlotte, Emily, Anne. At Haworth the accent is upon Brontë deaths (all the deaths are noted here except that of Anne, who died at Scarborough). The most joyous entry in the register relates to the marriage of Charlotte and Mr. Nicholls in 1854. It is sometimes on view, and visitors see the signatures of Charlotte's special friends, Ellen Nussey and Margaret Wooler, who were the witnesses.

In the Haworth registers are noted the burials of the two Brontë servants—Tabitha Aykroyd and Martha Brown. Their graves are outside the building in the chuchyard. Tabby was 84 years old when she died in February, 1855. Martha assisted her about the parsonage; she served Mr. Brontë and Mr. Nicholls and then when Mr. Nicholls, widower, left Haworth for Ireland she accompanied him. Mr. Nicholls married for a second time.

The Parsonage: It is not exactly as the Brontës knew it, for the Rev. John Wade's energies were not exhausted by the church rebuilding. He had enough energy left to extend the Georgian parsonage of 1779, and in 1872 a north and west wing were added. It is the first part of the building to be seen by those who approach the parsonage from the direction of the church, for it is adjacent to the road. As mentioned elsewhere, Mr. Brontë had made some modest additions to the rear of Haworth parsonage, and in recent times considerable extensions have taken place in this area by the Brontë Society.

Fortunately for those who admire the Brontës, the people of Haworth provided their rector with a new home. The old building was bought by Sir James Roberts, a native of the village, and he handed it over to the Brontë Society, the opening ceremony being performed by Lady Roberts in the August of 1928. The latest additions were much needed, allowing visitors to leave the building by a door other than the main entrance and providing accommodation for the custodian. The former custodian, Mrs. Joanna Hutton, supervised the conversion of the cellars of Haworth parsonage so that there is now room for talks on the Brontë family to be given to visiting parties.

The parsonage has altered in size, but not in spirit. Mr. Wade's new wing has long since mellowed to tone with the oldest part of the house. The extensions at the back are not seen by the majority of visitors and the approach from Haworth is one without a discordant note. Even the sign directing visitors to the front door is tasteful. It shows Charlotte sitting at a centre-leg table, with a paraffin lamp to provide the illumination as she writes. Designed by Mr. Harold G. Mitchell it was made in wrought-iron by the village blacksmith, Mr. Herbert Scarborough.

The garden is relatively small. In it are two fir trees, planted by Charlotte and her husband in 1854. They had just returned from their honeymoon. A flagged path leads to the main door. Martha Brown was to recall that Emily took her writing-desk and small buffet into the garden and ' in the shade of the trees, sat writing for hours together". Inside the parsonage the visitor tours rooms which the Brontës knew, for the wings erected in Mr. Wade's time are not normally open to view. Here is the office from which the affairs of the Brontë Society and of the museum are administered. Here, too, is a vast collection of books with Brontë links. They are made available to students who apply to the curator in advance.

Important objects in the museum have been cased in glass because of their delicacy and intrinsic value, but a sense of naturalness remains, particularly in the first two rooms which are seen — the dining-room and parlour, which flank the hall, being in keeping with the spirit of the early part of the 19th century. When it was meal time at Haworth Parsonage there was a notable absentee from the dining room, and that was Patrick Brontë, who preferred to dine alone in his study. The dining room's furnishings include the sofa on which Emily died.

The "study" was actually the parlour, but Mr. Brontë made it so much his own that his childen could not enter without special permission or if some very important matter had arisen. It has no incongruous object. Brooding over the room is the spirit of Mr. Brontë. You are directed to it by a fine portrait of the man above the fireplace and by a grouping of some of his treasures on the table—an open Bible, the spectacles he wore, his pipe, some matches and a tobacco box.

Mr. Nicholls had married Charlotte, but that did not automatically make him a bosom friend of the parson. He entered the study with courtesy and restraint, and he had his own special room in which he might study or write out his sermons. It was previously a storeroom, and Charlotte, Emily and Anne had once kept their two tame geese, Adelaide and Victoria, here. Charlotte converted it into a study in 1854, putting green and white curtains to the window and observing to her friend Ellen Nussey that they exactly suited the wallpaper. The room is seen by visitors to the parsonage, and just across the hall is the kitchen where objects that the Brontës would have known (toasting-iron, salt box, crimping-iron for pleating) are on view. The kitchen would be unfamiliar to them. Mr. Wade carried out considerable alterations in this area.

Upstairs at the Parsonage the distinctive characters of the Brontë family and their servants begin to reveal themselves. There is Tabby's Room, its scale and position in the house clearly reflecting the Victorian status of the hired help, though in fact the Brontë servants, in the absence of a mistress, played a not inconsiderable part in the growing-up of the children, and they were never treated with condescension. Charlotte's room is actually the area she and her husband occupied during their brief marriage, for previously it had been used by the stern but kindly Elizabeth Branwell, sister-in-law of Patrick Brontë, who kept an eye on the household for 21 years.

Emily's Room is the old nursery, the romping ground for the Brontë children and the place where they lived their rich life of make-believe, as revealed by the mass of manuscripts which date from their youthful years. As if a copious supply of paper was not enough, the children were fond of adorning the walls with tiny drawings. Emily occupied the room when the family was grown up. The menfolk slept in the room which is now called the Rev. P. Brontë's Room. Patrick and his son Branwell both died here. There is a room of special Branwell interest, featuring some of his paintings, and exhibition rooms at the rear (in that part of the house dating from 1872) include windows which were mentioned in Charlotte's novel *Shirley*.

The oldest part of the house has been left, but the Brontë spirit endures in the manuscripts of the Bonnell Collection (with a room to themselves) and in a bronze statue group of the three sisters, the work of Jocelyn Horner, which dominates the extension loggia. The group was cast in 1951.

The Black Bull: It is square and substantial, probably of 18th century date; it stands at the head of the steep main street, close to the church, and of all the people associated with it one name stands out sharply, and that is Branwell Brontë. The masonic lodge met here, and Branwell (as secretary) was always present. Later in life he frequented it without special reason except to

Haworth Parsonage, which was bought from the church by Sir James Roberts. He handed it over to the Brontë Society in 1928.

Left—Charlotte Brontë. Right—Emily Brontë as painted in oils by her brother Branwell (courtesy of the National Portrait Gallery).

The Rev. Patrick Brontë.

The Handwriting of
Father and Daughter

(Above: Rev. Patrick Brontë. Below: Charlotte.)

Above: Bronte Bridge, Haworth.

Opposite: Scenes in Haworth village.
(Photos: Clifford Robinson)

Left—The premises in Market Street, Thornton, which early last century housed the Brontës when Patrick was curate at the hillside village. Four of his children were born here.

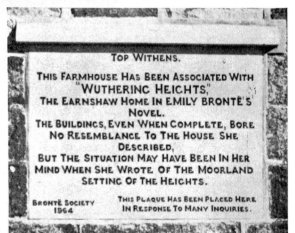

TOP WITHENS.

THIS FARMHOUSE HAS BEEN ASSOCIATED WITH "WUTHERING HEIGHTS," THE EARNSHAW HOME IN EMILY BRONTË'S NOVEL.

THE BUILDINGS, EVEN WHEN COMPLETE, BORE NO RESEMBLANCE TO THE HOUSE SHE DESCRIBED, BUT THE SITUATION MAY HAVE BEEN IN HER MIND WHEN SHE WROTE OF THE MOORLAND SETTING OF THE HEIGHTS.

BRONTË SOCIETY 1964

THIS PLAQUE HAS BEEN PLACED HERE IN RESPONSE TO MANY INQUIRIES.

Left: The Brontë Chair, near Haworth.

Above—Mrs. and the Rev. W. Carus Wilson, who opened a school at Cowen Bridge in 1824.

Left—The School, intended for daughters of the clergy. It was attended by the Brontë sisters.

Right—Martha Brown, servant of the Brontës at Haworth for many years.

Above: Jonas Bradley, of Stanbury.

Right: "Timmy Feather" (who died in 1910) outside his Stanbury cottage.

Haworth station yard. In the picture are some of the preservation society's engines and carriages on display.

drink and to express his strange personality in the company of others. Whatever his shortcomings, it is clear that Branwell Brontë was good company.

Drink and disease wasted him away, and there is a graphic account of him in *Pictures of the Past*, by F. H. Grundy (published in 1879). Mr. Grundy let the parsonage know that he was at the *Black Bull* and that dinner was being laid for himself and his friend Branwell, but he did not know that Branwell was very ill, lying in bed almost too weak to leave it.

It was typical of Branwell that he should accept his friend's invitation, especially

Haworth main street.

if it was at the *Black Bull*. Grundy recalled that "the door opened cautiously and a head appeared. It was a mass of red unkempt uncut hair, wildly floating round a great gaunt forehead; the cheeks yellow and hollow, the mouth fallen, the thin lips not trembling but shaking, the sunken eye, once small, now glaring with the light of madness." Whether Branwell enjoyed his meal or not is unknown. Caution at this stage of ill-health would not have helped him to avoid the inevitable. A few days after his journey from bed to the *Black Bull* the wild youth of Haworth Parsonage was dead.

Patrick Brontë took part in political meetings at the *Old White Lion*, an 18th century inn where a hoard of coins, including sovereigns and half sovereigns, has been found.

Sowdens: Of pre-Brontë interest, but a building which the Brontës would know well and which survives to give the atmosphere of their time. Its special association is with the Rev. William Grimshaw (1742-63), for it was his home, a place for prayer meetings and other religious gatherings.

4. Walks in Brontë Country

In fine and suitable weather delightful rambles were made over the moors and down into the glens and ravines that here and there broke the monotony of the moorland.

Ellen Nussey, Charlotte Brontë's friend.

I intended to have written a line yesterday, but just as I was sitting down for that purpose, Arthur called to me to take a walk. We set off, not intending to go far; but though wild and cloudy it was fine in the morning; when we had got about half-a-mile on the moors, Arthur suggested the idea of the waterfall; after the melted snow, he said it would be fine. I had often wished to see it in its winter power, so we walked on. It was fine indeed; a perfect torrent racing over the rocks, white and beautiful.

Charlotte to a friend, 1854.

THE FIRST WALK: TO THE BRONTË FALLS

(2¼ miles from Haworth)

A SIGNPOST at Haworth once directed visitors "To the Cemetery and Waterfall", and there is a grimness about the association. The quotation above, from Charlotte's letter to a friend, deals with a walk which was possibly the last long walk that Charlotte took. She had a weak constitution, and was not very well when she returned, experiencing a shiver and then a bad lingering sore throat and cold, which hung about her, making her thin and weak. She died the following spring.

Early writers about the Brontës tended to dwell overmuch on the distances that were covered and on the severity of the ground. They were apt to be overawed by the moors which, though they must always be treated with respect, are not some vast tundra set down in England. Mrs. Gaskell, who gave us details of Charlotte's walk, mentioned a distance of seven or eight miles when, in fact, it is less than five miles there and back. The Brontë Waterfall to be seen at the end of the walk out from Haworth is no Niagara (Whiteley Turner, writing in 1913, referred to "a mere trickle of water amid moss-covered rocks") but it was undoubtedly well-loved by the Brontë children and, to understand their work (particularly the prose and verse of Emily) an expedition to the waterfall is valuable.

Some of the sense of adventure was stripped from the most-used route to the Brontë waterfalls when a hard surface was laid along the old footpath to allow motor vehicles to be driven to Far Intake. Anyone who takes a car thus far will have only one mile of walking left, on a pleasant rough path fringed with heather and bracken.

For the walker from Haworth, the instructions are relatively simple. Leave the village by West Lane, and a left turn should be made at the end of the lane, where a signpost is inscribed "Brontë Falls". The way lies close to the village cemetery and soon *Hill Top Cafe* (a white building) is seen on the right.

At a junction with the reservoir road (which descends fairly steeply and crosses the embankment of Lower Laithe Reservoir to reach the Haworth-Stanbury road) continue walking straight ahead (signpost $1\frac{1}{2}$ miles) along the metalled road (single track) to Far Intake, now unoccupied. The heather, mainly the commonest variety, ling, is on the left, and there are fields to the right. August and September are the months when the normally drab moorland is purpled by heather blossom. The bee-keepers of Haworth district took their hives to the moors so that they could make good use of this last great show of blossom in the year. Heather honey, dark and viscid, is not to everyone's taste, being rather strong.

From Far Intake a rough track continues, descending to Sladen Beck and the Falls. Before reaching the bridge, the first item of interest is the so-called Brontë Chair of natural stone weathered and worn into the rough form of a seat. It faces up the moorland ravine towards the Falls, and no doubt was a favourite place of the Brontë sisters. There is some beauty in the waterfalls but it is not the beauty that overawes. The water descends in a series of small cascades whose volume is a faithful reflection of the weather, rain or drought. The other main feature of the area is the well-worn Brontë Bridge which crosses the Sladen Beck. It is a "clapper" type of bridge, of rough-hewn slabs of millstone grit, set on stone uprights.

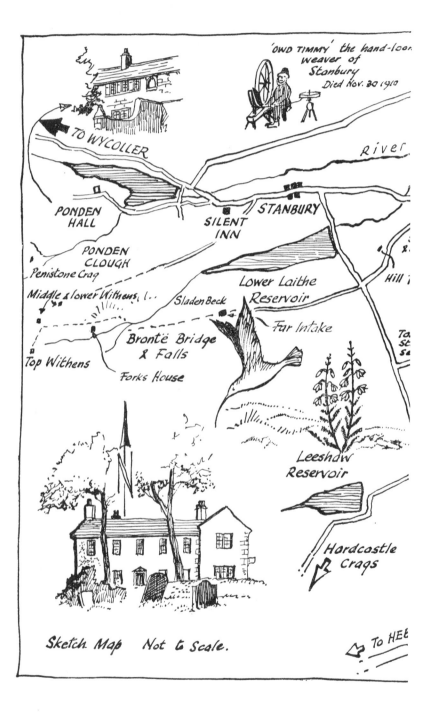

'OWD TIMMY' the hand-loom weaver of Stanbury
Died Nov. 30 1910

TO WYCOLLER

River

PONDEN HALL

STANBURY

SILENT INN

PONDEN CLOUGH

Penistone Crag

Hill

Middle & lower Withens

Sladen Beck

Lower Laithe Reservoir

Far Intake

Brontë Bridge & Falls

Top Withens

Forks House

Leeshaw Reservoir

Hardcastle Craqs

Sketch Map   Not to Scale.

To HEB

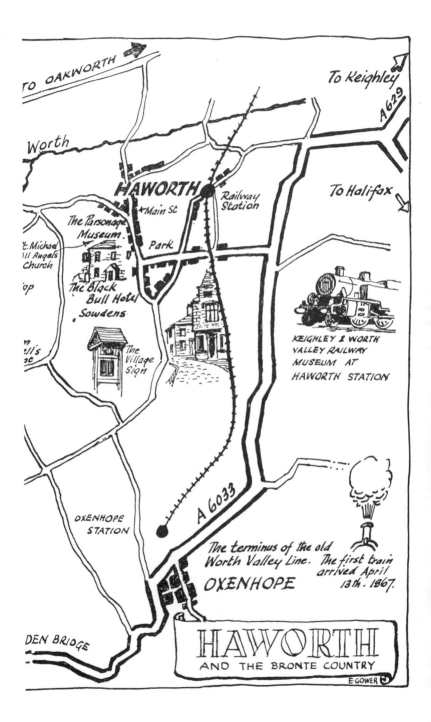

TO OAKWORTH

To Keighley

A629

Worth

HAWORTH

Main St

Railway Station

The Parsonage Museum

To Halifax

t. Michael ll Angels Church

Park

op

The Black Bull Hotel

Sowdens

The Village Sign

KEIGHLEY & WORTH VALLEY RAILWAY MUSEUM AT HAWORTH STATION

A 6033

OXENHOPE STATION

The terminus of the old Worth Valley Line. The first train arrived April 13th. 1867.

OXENHOPE

DEN BRIDGE

HAWORTH
AND THE BRONTE COUNTRY

E. GOWER

THE SECOND WALK: TO TOP WITHENS

(a little more than three miles from Haworth, and about a mile from the Brontë Waterfalls)

THIS is a natural extension of the walk to the Waterfalls. Cross the Brontë Bridge and follow the footpath which runs up the hillside, to the left of the derelict Virginia Farm which you will see on the skyline. In fine weather it is possible to walk straight ahead for a quarter of a mile to join the Stanbury-Withens moorland track, Top Withens being visible as you look ahead up the road. In inclement weather it is advisable to follow the footpath at the rear of the ruined Virginia Farm; continue through the yard of the next farm (Hill End Farm), also derelict, and join the track for Withens near a wooden gate across the road, turning left and proceeding along this track up the moor to the former Isolation Hospital, and Withens.

For years, Brontë students have speculated on the site of Emily's Wuthering Heights, and Top Withens has been mentioned most often in this connection. A stone plaque has been erected on the ruined building by the Brontë Society to denote that it might be the probable site. Readers of the novel who visit Top Withens may be moved at the thought of Isabella's sufferings in that household; others, seeing what is just one of many small sheep farms (now in a very sad state of ruin), wonder where the corn and hayfields of Wuthering Heights have gone, and what has happened to the garden of the house. Ponden Hall has been mentioned as a better Wuthering Heights than Top Withens, and writers have directed attention to the big room with the kitchen on the other side of the passage and to the large outbuildings.

A very good claim could be made for High Sunderland Hall, which Emily may have transported to the site of Top Withens. She had stayed at Miss Patchett's school at nearby Law Hill, and she would often see the ornate hall which was demolished in recent times. Before the demolition it was seen to conform very closely with the description given at the beginning of *Wuthering Heights*, where Mr. Lockwood first describes its front.

From Top Withens many people enjoy walking on an alternative footpath which leads back to Haworth via Stanbury, taking in Top, Middle and Lower Withens (only the foundations remain of the last two named). Follow the line of the farms down to Stanbury.

The Brontë Bridge near Haworth.

THE THIRD WALK:
TO PONDEN KIRK, "PENISTONE CRAG"

(about three miles, via Stanbury Moor)

START from Stanbury. A motorist can reach this village from Haworth in very short time via West Lane but by turning right to the Colne Road instead of going by Haworth Moor. From Stanbury, walk through the village and down the steep hill at the end, passing on the left a building, previously the *Eagle Inn* and featured by Halliwell Sutcliffe as the *Silent Inn* in his novel *Ricroft of Withens*. Cross Ponden Beck by the bridge, and turn immediately left, walking past Ponden Mill and by the rough road left of Ponden Reservoir.

Ponden Hall (on the right) was the Thrushcross Grange of *Wuthering Heights*. Robert Heaton built it for his son Michael in the first half of the 17th century, and later additions were made up to 1801. Significantly, 1801 is the year in which Emily Brontë's Wuthering tale began.

The road beyond the Hall is walled on either side until a gate is reached. There is open heath beyond. Take a left turning and pass two derelict farms at Upper Ponden. Ponden Kirk is at the crest of the ridge overlooking the valley (Ponden Clough). It can also be reached from Ponden Hall by Ponden Clough Valley and climbing about 200 steps of natural rock, a feat of agility for older people.

There is nothing ecclesiastical about Ponden Kirk—just a natural stone outcrop with a hole through which a reasonably agile person could scramble. There was a tradition that if a single woman crept through this hole she would be married within the year.

Turn to the moor again and follow the Ponden Clough Beck for almost a mile. Here are the Alcomden Stones, a Druidical-type of circle of large upright millstone grit stones, with a long view of the Halifax reservoirs down the Walshaw valley. The return to Stanbury is made by the same route as the outward journey, but it can be varied slightly by returning via Top Withens. This means crossing the moor in a southerly direction for half a mile or so, but as there is no official path across the moor from Ponden Kirk to Top Withens care is again advised.

THE FOURTH WALK: TOM STELL'S SEAT

(a short expedition of about one hour's duration)

TOM STELL was a rambler who, like the late Jonas Bradley, had a special affection for the Haworth moors, which he knew in all weathers. On the Stanbury-Oxenhope road, standing on a knoll which commands a great sweep of moorland a short distance from Haworth, is the memorial stone seat provided by his friends. Tom Stell is simply described as one who "loved these moors".

Leave Haworth by West Lane and the moor road on the left, as for the Brontë Falls. At the cross roads just beyond *Hill Top Cafe,* turn left and up the rise. Tom Stell's Seat is a quarter of a mile along the road on the left, and the panoramic view covers five moors—Brow, Oxenhope, Haworth, Stanbury and Oakworth. Continue down the road towards Oxenhope. The return may be made by turning left in half a mile at the first T-junction, through the hamlet of Higher Marsh, at the end of which Haworth Moor can be reached in one mile by proceeding straight ahead.

Alternatively the right fork can be taken. At the bend of the road in a quarter of a mile, there is a field path on the left which proceeds to Haworth churchyard, passing near Sowdens Farm (first farm on left, with path to left). A plaque on the wall commemorates the farm's former association with Haworth parsons, notably William Grimshaw. It is only five minutes' walk to Haworth church from that point.

THE FIFTH WALK: TO WYCOLLER

(rather more than seven miles from Haworth)

WYCOLLER Hall is ruined now. The roof fell in many years ago, and some of the walls are in a crumbling state. Yet this "Ferndean Manor" of Jane Eyre has a quiet greystone dignity even in ruin. The hall has been uninhabited since Brontë times (when Charlotte examined it the signs of decay were apparent), and had its greatest days in the latter part of the 16th century. The Hartleys, and later the Cunliffes, lived in the hall and managed its estates. The last of the Cunliffes died here at the time the Brontë family lived at Thornton.

In a bedroom of Wycoller Hall a Cunliffe gratified his love of the sport of cock-fighting. In Harland and Wilkinson's *Traditions of Lancashire* it is stated that once every year a spectral horse-man visits the building. He is attired in the costume of the early Stuart period, and the trappings of his horse are tattered. On the evening of his visit the weather is always wild and tempestuous. There is no moon to light the lonely roads, and the inhabitants do not venture out of their cottages. When the wind howls loudest the horseman can be heard dashing up the road at full speed; after crossing the narrow bridge, he suddenly stops at the door of the hall and, dismounting, makes his way up the broad oak stairs into one of the rooms of the house. Dreadful screams, as from a woman, are shortly heard, which soon subside into groans. The horseman then makes his reappearance at the door, at once mounts his steed, and gallops away on the same road.

The tradition is that one of the Cunliffes murdered his wife in that room, and that the spectral horseman is the ghost of the murderer, who is doomed to pay an annual visit to the house of his victim. Years before it actually happened, the murdered lady had predicted the extinction of her husband's race. The lady's prediction appears to have been literally fulfilled, for the last of the Cunliffes died at Wycoller in the year 1818. He was a lonely man, and the ancestral home soon became a ruin. What could Emily Brontë have made of such a tale?

Wycoller is one of the quiet hamlets, tucked out of sight of the modern world and out of hearing of most of its strident sounds. Here a lover of the works of the Brontës can feel an atmosphere to match the novels. It is a hamlet with a stream, and bridges of seven different types have been built across the water. In Charlotte's day also the area was well wooded. When Jane Eyre arrived at Ferndean Manor she discovered that it was "a building of considerable antiquity, moderate size and no architectural pretentions, deep buried in a wood".

Most visitors nowadays arrive at Wycoller by car, which is a pity for them. They miss the essential contemplation as the hamlet draws near, and within it there is concern about turning the car or parking it. Jane Eyre performed the last mile of her journey on foot and "even when within a very short distance of the manor-house you could see nothing of it, so thick and dark grew the timber of the gloomy wood about it." Wycoller is still entered with some surprise because of its position deep in a little valley, with winding approach roads.

The best footway from Haworth is over the main motor road

The hamlet of Wycoller, where Charlotte's best-known novel, "Jane Eyre",
was set. Here stood "Ferndean Manor".

through Stanbury (a mile from Haworth), past the *Silent Inn* and Ponden reservoir to the top of the steep Two Laws Hill and its junction with the Oakworth-Colne road. Here turn left to pass Moor Lodge (a shooting lodge), and eventually Water Sheddles reservoir is reached. Just before coming to a keeper's cottage beyond the reservoir there is a gate on the left opposite a stone seat bearing the inscription "Rest awhile". This marks the beginning of the delightful bridle path down through Wycoller Dene to the hall.

For those not wishing to walk back to Haworth, the return journey may be made by 'bus from Laneshaw Bridge (1 mile) via Keighley; thence by 'bus to Haworth.

Water from the high land around Haworth flows into several reservoirs, and the catchment area is normally out of bounds, apart from the well-used footpaths which have been mentioned in this section. The reservoirs and much of the land is controlled by the district Water Board, which has offices in Skipton. The Board can provide specific information about rights on its territories.

Extra care should be taken during the shooting season from August 12th onwards. Moor fires could occur through careless-ness with matches and cigarettes. During misty weather caution is required, especially in the higher altitudes, such as the Withens and Ponden Kirk areas, where there are many streams and considerable areas of bog.

5. Places known to the Brontës

COWAN BRIDGE, on the A65 between Ingleton and Kirkby Lonsdale. Here the Brontë girls attended the Clergy Daughters' School of the Rev. W. Carus-Wilson:

THE school was founded and opened in January, 1824, and Maria and Elizabeth Brontë arrived here in July of the same year. Charlotte was sent to Cowan Bridge in August, and Emily followed in November. A house had been adapted for the use of the teachers, and on to it was built a long annexe in which the pupils had their lessons by day and their sleep at night. The school was possibly no worse than dozens of others in the North at that time, but it had grim memories for the Brontë children, and particularly for Charlotte. She later described it under the name of Lowood in *Jane Eyre.*

The Brontë children did not see Cowan Bridge at its best; they lived here through the winter and were hastily taken back to Haworth in the spring of 1825 when there was an outbreak of low fever. Maria and then Elizabeth were first sent home (the fever, affecting their already weak constitutions, caused their deaths). Charlotte and Emily stayed on a little longer.

Picture the Brontë girls with thick winter wear of purple dresses and short capes. For days that were cold and wet they wore green plaid cloaks and pattens. Brown holland pinafores were worn on weekdays, and they donned white pinafores on Sundays. Church attendance meant a two-and-a-half miles walk to Tunstall Church.

The school was later moved to Casterton, near Kirkby Lonsdale and is now one of the best-known girls' schools in the North. At Cowan Bridge the school was converted into three cottages, on the gable end of which is a commemorative plaque: "At this school Maria, Elizabeth, Charlotte, Emily, daughters of the Rev. P. Brontë, were educated in 1824-25."

THE COVE, SILVERDALE, the seaside home of the Rev. W. Carus-Wilson:

Charlotte and Emily were sent here after the outbreak of fever at Cowan Bridge, but they stayed for only one night. The bedroom where they slept became known as the Brontë Room. The

Cove is now a fellowship centre. Also of Brontë interest at Silverdale is Gibraltar, a building with a stout castellated tower which is seen by those who walk to Jenny Brown's Point. Mrs. Gaskell, Charlotte's biographer, was a visitor to Gibraltar. It is said that she sat in the tower to watch Morecambe Bay's celebrated sunsets.

ROE HEAD, near Gomersal, where Charlotte was first a pupil and later a governess:

Roe Head was then a school run by the Misses Wooler. Charlotte first arrived here in January, 1831, and she met her lifelong friends Ellen Nussey and Mary Taylor. She was at Roe Head for only 18 months, returning to Haworth to teach her sisters. She was back again in July, 1835, and this time Emily travelled with her. Homesick, Emily returned to Haworth after two months, her place being taken by Anne. Charlotte finally left this school in May, 1838.

LAW HILL, Southowram, where Emily was a governess:

Miss Patchett had run a school at Law Hill. Emily arrived in October, 1837.

STONE GAPPE, Lothersdale, near Cross Hills, which was Gateshead Hall in "Jane Eyre":

Charlotte visited Stone Gappe in the restless period between schooling and serious writing. She became a governess with the Sidgwicks, and stayed here for less than three months. Lady Wilson, of Eshton Hall, told a meeting of the Brontë Society in the 1930s: "I cannot help feeling at times a grain of pity for those unfortunate ladies who chartered a Brontë for service in their schoolrooms. Always trailing their thread-bare but neatly-darned cloaks in quest of real or fancied insults, out of sympathy with their charges, devoid or almost devoid of the saving grace of humour, and filled with a nostalgic desire for their own home, they must surely have been a severe trial to their employers." In short, they were never very happy as governesses.

SCARBOROUGH, St. Mary's Churchyard:

The burial place of Anne, who died at Scarborough aged 29 years in May, 1849. Charlotte took her to this resort on the East Coast, where it was believed the air would do her good, but she died within a few days.

GAWTHORPE HALL, near Burnley, the home of Sir James Kay-Shuttleworth and Lady Shuttleworth:

They were contemporaries of Charlotte Brontë who admired her work. The Rev. Patrick Brontë was greatly touched when they visited the Parsonage at Haworth, and Charlotte was at

Gawthorpe Hall in March, 1850. It was the prelude to her first visit to the Lake District in the summer of the same year. The Shuttleworths had rented Briery Close, on the shore of Windermere. Another guest was Mrs. Gaskell, and Charlotte met her for the first time.

Among the Lakeland homes visited by Charlotte was The Knoll, Ambleside, where Miss Harriet Martineau lived. Charlotte had been introduced to Miss Martineau in London in 1849, and they were re-acquainted in the North in 1850. Miss Martineau recorded that a young-looking lady in deep mourning, neat as a Quaker, with beautiful brown hair, great blazing eyes and a sensible face showing self-control, appeared at the door, hesitating to find four or five people, looked round and then went straight to Miss Martineau and sheltered near her with childlike confidence.

STANBURY, close to Haworth, which the Brontës knew only as visitors. It would be a familiar sight to them as they took the moorland tracks from home.

Near this straggling village, beside the Haworth-Colne road, was the home of Timmy Feather, who is described as "the last of the handloom weavers". Here, too, lived one of the most knowledgeable of the Brontë-lovers, Jonas Bradley, who was born two years before the death of the Rev. Patrick Brontë. Jonas lived for 84 years. He had no great success at his chosen career of schoolmaster (if judged by academic standards) but he was one of the pioneers of teaching out-of-doors.

Jonas Bradley was a founder member of the Brontë Society and he was recognised at that time as an authority on the subject. Visitors to the Haworth district from many parts of the world sought him out. He spoke about the Brontës with a sound sense at a time of outrageous romanticism. His favourite was Emily, and he defended her against an attack by an American writer. He maintained that Mrs. Gaskell had done an injustice to Patrick Brontë in her pen portrait of him. He was equally forthright in his defence of Branwell Brontë, maintaining that a wrong impression had been given. Jonas Bradley once said: "There must have been something nice about him, otherwise Emily would not have been so fond of him. He went wrong because of uncongenial surroundings."

Today, many people who study the Brontës closely are giving most credit to Emily, possibly the only member of the Brontë family with real genius as compared with the high degree of talent shown by her sister Charlotte. In this, Jonas Bradley was very perceptive. He lived rather too close to the Brontë age for real assessment, and nothing that has been written since has thrown much favourable light upon Branwell.

6. The Novels of the Brontës

If the Brontës' novels be subjected to a critical inquiry as to the kind and degree of impression which they make upon the reader, they emerge as unique in kind and very high intensity. Their stories, characters, settings and points of view are entirely original, while the strange pungent blend of Celtic poetry and sardonic Yorkshire realism in which they are presented is not to be found in any other novel.

Dr. Phyllis Bentley.

Girls, do you know Charlotte has been writing a book, and it is much better than likely?

Rev. Patrick Brontë, on reading "Jane Eyre".

CHARLOTTE, Emily and Anne Brontë published a book of their verse in 1846. The printer's bill came to £50, and two copies of the book were sold. Maybe they would have done better if their real names had been known, for there was some loyalty to the Parsonage. Instead they chose pen-names—Currer, Ellis and Acton Bell—which cloaked their identity while preserving their initials.

That same year they took to writing novels—or, as Charlotte put it, prose tales. It was agreed among them that once again their writing would be under aliases. The books were written against the despondency of the failure of their verse, against the sorrows at home (notably the wild ways of Branwell) and against the strangeness of the novel form. They had been accustomed to scribbling stories for years, but the writing of extended tales for possible publication called from them all their resources of spirit and stamina. In their favour was the general literary background of the Parsonage (Patrick Brontë was fond of books, tried his hand at writing and was a keen supporter of local town libraries), and the continuous interest and support each received from the others. Charlotte, Emily and Anne might each write in solitude, but they enjoyed talking about their projects and reading from them.

Charlotte had written *The Professor*. If she sometimes fumbled for the right words, the emotions were easily roused, for this book was firmly based upon her experiences in Brussels, with the personalities but thinly disguised. In Brussels, Charlotte had been the pupil-teacher—a shy, fumbling girl from a Yorkshire village set down in the company of the more worldly M. Heger, who assisted his wife in running a private school for girls. Charlotte fell deeply in love with M. Heger; he was kindly towards her but there is no reason to believe that the love was reciprocated, and behind it all was the ominous figure of Madame Heger. At no other time in Charlotte's life was her love so heartfelt or—in the light of its impossibility of being returned—was the subsequent bitterness so raw.

The love flowered again in *The Professor*, but the Yorkshire visitor to Brussels was a man, William Crimsworth, who taught in a boys' school (run by M. Pelet) and the adjacent girls' school (Mlle Zoraide Reuter). Crimsworth loved Francis Henri, a young pupil-teacher (Charlotte yearned to be loved by M. Heger). The bitterness of those Brussels days flowered again—such a bitterness that publishers who read the book winced and hurriedly posted it back to Haworth; such a realism that the literary world was not quite ready for it. It would be published after Charlotte's death.

Emily Brontë's deepest feelings were bared in *Wuthering Heights*. Emotions which she had to repress to conform to the image of a village parson's daughter came bubbling to the surface as she told the strange, astonishing story of the Earnshaws of Wuthering Heights and the Lintons of Thrushcross Grange, but most particularly of the uninhibited animal love of Heathcliff for Catherine. "Wuthering" in the dialect of the Pennines means "storming"—the roar of the north wind across a moorland ridge; the deep blue storm clouds, crackling with thunder and the vivid lightning flashes, touching the earth to burn the peat and fill the air with a sulphurous tang. The weather which Emily Brontë knew on her Yorkshire moors was rarely settled, and something of its spirit is captured by the interplay of the characters in the book. *Wuthering Heights* is a love story—a love story such as had never been told before, savage and passionate in its splendour but unfulfilled at the end.

No one pretends that it is the best-constructed novel that has been penned. Emily had never written a novel before, and there is some clumsiness in the way the story is told. It is not the best-written novel, and generally its style is far too pedantic for its success to be based simply upon the use of words. *Wuthering Heights* stands out in the history of English literature (and some would claim that it is unexcelled) because of its striking originality and timelessness. A young woman who was acutely shy and homesick, who revelled in her own company and yet felt the sting of loneliness, who felt most elated when out on the moors, with the primeval forces of nature about her, turned out a prose tale which has remained unique and one of the most striking reflections of the make-up of a writer that has been presented.

Anne worked at a novel called *Agnes Grey*. She drew deeply on the experiences which the Brontë sisters could best appreciate —the arrival of a governess at a strange house and her relationship with her employer and his family. Anne's was a quietly-told tale compared with the stories of Charlotte and Emily, but it was deeply felt, and especially the love which the governess felt for a curate—a love which might have been an echo of Anne's own feelings for one of the young men who assisted her father at Haworth.

Few masterpieces of prose can have had rougher treatment than the novels sent out by the Brontës. They went together and then in separate parcels to different publishers. They returned to the Parsonage with a wearying regularity. One publisher, named Newby, was not highly regarded in the world of print. The almost-despairing Emily and Anne were relieved when he agreed to accept their novels—even when he asked for £50 towards the cost of publication. Charlotte had to wait a little longer. Then a Mr. Williams, reader with the firm of Smith, Elder and Company in Paternoster Row, London, was attracted to the work. This did not stop the firm sending back the manuscript, but with it went a letter which promised that careful consideration would be given to another work from the same pen.

Charlotte had already begun work on another novel. It was to be her best-loved, best-remembered story, *Jane Eyre*, in which she drew deeply on her experiences as a governess and revealed the peculiar heartache which the Brontë girls must have felt when they were in the service of others. Emily had her Heathcliff, and now Charlotte presented a man with the same animal instincts in Rochester. The central figure of Jane suggests Charlotte herself—a very plain Jane doing the right things in disorderly circumstances, yearning for a love which (it seems) will never come but finding a response to it at the very end in a marriage to the wreck of the man who had been Rochester. There is drama in the mad exploits of Rochester's wife, in the fire she starts; excitement and suspense in the story of the locked room and in many of the incidents of a neatly-told story.

Jane Eyre was born in worry and concern. Charlotte went to Manchester with her father, who was to have an operation for the removal of a cataract from an eye. It was a chancy operation then, and it cannot have helped Charlotte's peace of mind to witness it. The surgeon operated on Patrick Brontë in the bedroom of the house where they were staying, and there was no anaesthetic to dull the pain. Charlotte had slept little because of worry and also because of an aching tooth. On the morning of the operation her manuscript of *The Professor* returned yet again (at this stage it had not been submitted to Smith, Elder and Company). *Jane Eyre* was completed in the summer of 1847, and the publishers did not dawdle with the manuscript. Eight weeks after they received it, the book was ready for sale. The public liked it, and the first edition was quickly sold out.

Newby, the publisher with the works of Emily and Anne, saw his chance of cashing in on the fame of *Jane Eyre*, and soon *Wuthering Heights* and *Agnes Grey* were available. Smith, Elder and Company had made a first-rate job of *Jane Eyre* (Charlotte, acknowledging six copies of the book, wrote that "you have given the work every advantage which good paper, clear type and a seemly outside can supply") but Newby's products were poorly made and had hardly any impact on the literary circles of the time.

For a while there was confusion. The novels appeared with the surname Bell. There was a belief that all had been written by the same hand. The authorship was a close secret which not even Patrick Brontë shared. He first saw *Jane Eyre* when it was well into its second edition. The confusion ended suddenly in the summer of 1848, when Newby was reported to have sold the American rights of a new book by the author of *Jane Eyre* (this was, in fact Anne's second novel, *The Tenant of Wildfell Hall*). Smith, Elder and Company, having the rights on Charlotte's work, were annoyed and they wrote to her about it. Charlotte and Anne made the long, then difficult journey to London. The letter established Charlotte's identity and gave Smith, Elder the shock of finding that their best-selling author was a woman. Later the Brontës agreed that their identities should be generally known.

Jane Eyre had been written during one of Charlotte's darkest hours. Her third book, *Shirley*, was prepared in circumstances which would have deranged many people. Over 20 years had gone by since the deaths of Mrs. Brontë, Elizabeth and Maria. Between September, 1848, and May, 1849, there was a trio of deaths—first Branwell, then Emily and Anne. Branwell was no great loss to Charlotte, for her sisterly feelings had long since been blunted by his wildness and excesses. Emily and Anne had been close to her, and of the two Charlotte had a specially deep love for Emily, who became the character behind the name of *Shirley*.

Patrick Brontë was not the most affectionate of fathers, but when he was not pre-occupied by parish matters he could excite his children with tales of the past: of cabin life in Ireland and the days of the troubles when he first arrived in the West Riding. He told of the manufacturers who built themselves large mills for power looms, and of the men, jobless or fretful at the possibility of losing work in the old handcraft sense, who banded themselves together as the Luddites, taking a solemn pledge to smash the machines. Patrick Brontë was possibly a better storyteller than a writer, and certainly much of what he told his daughters was used in their books. Charlotte, recalling the Calder Valley of 1812, and the turbulence at the Rawford Mills when two men died, wove her last story around them. Maybe she brooded a little too much on what Emily might have been had she lived, for there was a split interest, with two heroines, Caroline and Shirley. When the novel was begun, Charlotte had the company of her sisters; when its writing was completed she had only her father left in the immediate family.

In public she was being carried along on a tidal wave of popularity, and the success of *Shirley* was assured. Charlotte did not court success; she remained a shy, self-conscious person, physically weak, so buffeted by tragedies close at hand that an air of weary sadness was hanging over her. *The Professor* was still unsold, but Charlotte must return to the memories of Brussels for the material that could be used in her next book, *Villette*. The Hegers were still alive, and it is likely that news of the literary success of their erstwhile pupil had reached them. What came as a great shock was *Villette*, for into it Charlotte recounted her life in Brussels, and the bitter sweetness of her feelings for M. Heger with such direct frankness that the Hegers felt a shiver of embarrassment when they had the opportunity of reading it.

Charlotte began to write *Villette* in 1850, and eight years had gone by since she first met M. Heger. In those eight years the mind had a better opportunity of sifting and correlating what she had felt and done than at the time of her first impetuous excursion into the novel form with *The Professor*. In addition, Charlotte's mind and body were being slowed down by ill-health (she wondered in 1851 how she had managed to get through the winter), and the writing of *Villette* was prolonged, lasting through that year, through another bitter winter, and on to the end of 1852. It was published in the following year. When Charlotte Brontë died she had begun a fifth novel.

7. Brontë Personalities

(in alphabetical order)

AYKROYD, Tabitha, known to the Brontës as "Tabby". She was the servant who arrived at Haworth Parsonage in 1825 and was still in Brontë employ when she died in February, 1855, aged 84 years. Her grave is in the old churchyard at Haworth, close up against the Parsonage wall.

BELL, Miss Mary. The cousin of the Rev. Arthur Bell Nicholls, curate at Haworth who became the husband of Charlotte Brontë. Charlotte met Mary Bell once, when she was on her honeymoon in Ireland, visiting the old homes of Mr. Nicholls at Banagher. When the bereaved Mr. Nicholls returned to Ireland it was to Banagher—and to eventual marriage with Mary Bell.

BROWN, Martha. Brontë servant, who took up her duties in 1838 and was still at the parsonage on the death of Patrick Brontë in 1861. Martha Brown accompanied the Rev. Arthur Bell Nicholls when he moved back to Ireland.

GASKELL, Mrs., the biographer of Charlotte Brontë. Her *Life* was published in 1857, and she compiled it at the invitation of Patrick Brontë. Elizabeth Cleghorn Gaskell was born in 1810 and died in 1865.

HEGER, M. Constantin, Roman Catholic who with his wife ran a Brussels school for girls. Charlotte Brontë went to the school in 1842, with Emily as a companion, seeking to improve her knowledge of foreign languages which would be of benefit to her in teaching. She fell in love with M. Heger. A second visit to the Brussels school took place, this time with Charlotte as a pupil-teacher. M. Heger died in May, 1896. Letters that Charlotte wrote to him were given to the British Museum by Dr. Heger, his son, in 1913.

HOUGHTON, Lord. First president of the Brontë Society, which was formed in 1893, and is now the oldest of the English Literary Societies, with a present membership of 1,600, over 350 of them in America. The Society administers the Parsonage Museum at Haworth, which is visited by over 200,000 people a year.

HUDSON, Mrs., of Easton, Bridlington. A friend of Charlotte who was her hostess when she and Ellen Nussey visited Bridlington in September, 1839. There was a second visit by Charlotte in June, 1849, and while she was at Bridlington she wrote part of her novel *Shirley*.

INGRAM, Mrs., Anne's employer at Blake Hall, Mirfield, from April, 1838 to December of the same year. Anne was engaged as governess.

KAY-SHUTTLEWORTH, Sir James and Lady. Friends of Charlotte who lived at Gawthorpe Hall, Lancashire. They entertained Charlotte at Gawthorpe, and she later stayed with them at Briery Close, Westmorland, in 1850. It was at Briery Close that Charlotte met Mrs. Gaskell.

NICHOLLS, Rev. Arthur Bell, the husband of Charlotte Brontë. He was an Irishman who became acquainted with her when curate at Haworth; his proposal of marriage was treated with ridicule and contempt by Patrick Brontë, but he relented and the ceremony took place at Haworth Church in June, 1854. On the death of Mr. Brontë he retired to Ireland, where he married again. He died in 1906.

NUSSEY, ELLEN, lifelong friend of Charlotte Brontë. They regularly corresponded, and Miss Nussey kept most of the letters, against the wishes of the Rev. A. B. Nicholls. They provide a valuable insight into the Brontë period. Ellen Nussey was the bridesmaid when Charlotte was married in 1854.

PATCHETT, Miss, who had a school at Law Hill, Southowram, Halifax. Emily was a governess here for a short period beginning in October, 1837.

ROBINSON, Mrs., of Thorp Green Hall, Little Ouseburn, where Anne was a governess from March, 1841, until June, 1845, and Branwell was tutor from January, 1843, to July, 1845.

SIDGWICK, Mrs., of Stone Gappe, Lothersdale. Charlotte was a governess here from May, 1839 until July of the same year.

SMITH, George, principal of the publishing firm of Smith, Elder and Company. He was one of Charlotte's several suitors.

SOWDEN, the Rev. Sutcliffe. He performed the wedding ceremony when Charlotte Brontë married Arthur Bell Nicholls in 1854.

TAYLOR, Mary, one of Charlotte's few real friends, from a meeting at Miss Wooler's School at Roe Head until her death.

WEIGHTMAN, Rev. William. A curate at Haworth from August 1839. He died in 1842. The time when Weightman was a regular visitor at the parsonage was one of special pleasure for the Brontë family and particularly the Brontë sisters, because of his jolly, lighthearted ways.

WOOLER, Miss Margaret, who with her sister had the school at Roe Head. She gave Charlotte away at her wedding.

Roe Head, where Charlotte was a pupil for 18 months from 1831, and where she taught from 1835 to 1838. The building is now a school run by the Verona Fathers.

8. A Railway came to Haworth

They had a meetin' t'other neet,
Fair oth top o' wutherin street,
To see what things they'd got complete,
Concerning Haworth railway.

Bill o'th' Hoylus End, 1886.

WHEN Charlotte and Anne Brontë travelled to London to meet the publishers Smith, Elder and Company, their luggage was moved by cart to the railway station at Keighley and the young women followed on foot. It was not a pleasant journey because of fierce summer storms. A train from Keighley delivered them, weary and crumpled, to a London just awakening to another day. The Brontës lived at the time of the railway mania, the 1840s. Charlotte's novel *Jane Eyre* was published in 1847, the year when the Midland Railway Company opened the railway line from Shipley to Skipton. The tracks were just nicely bedded in when Charlotte and Anne made their London trip.

In the 1840s there were some wild schemes for railways and for a time money was not in short supply to finance the most reasonable of them. Promoters thought of possible lucrative lines between the industrialised West Riding and the equally well-developed East Lancashire. One idea was for a railway to Colne, via Cross Hills and Cowling. Another foresaw a steam service to Colne from Keighley via Watersheddles, Trawden and Laneshaw Bridge, which would have meant a great viaduct across the Worth Valley from Cross Roads to Haworth and—perhaps—a station at Stanbury! Both projects were abandoned.

There were mill and property owners in the Worth Valley who would benefit from a railway. It was decided among them that a purely local venture would be made. Fifteen years of negotiation were required before an Act of Parliament received Royal sanction authorising the building of a Worth Valley line. When the negotiations began Charlotte Brontë had the printed version of *Shirley* before her and during a visit to London she met the mighty Thackeray. As talk about the railway went wearily on, Charlotte married—and died; Mrs. Gaskell began her researches into the Brontës, and Mr. Nicholls added a preface to Charlotte's first novel, *The Professor*, which was published in 1857. When the first sod on the Worth Valley line was cut in February, 1865, all the Brontës were dead and Mr. Nicholls lived in Ireland. The railway catered for the many curious people who, having read the works of the Brontës, wanted to see the actual places which the talented sisters had known.

Mr. (later Sir) Isaac Holden cut the first sod. Keighley had suggested that the ceremony should be on April 1st, but Haworth objected. They did not want to be considered April fools. The date when Mr. Holden wielded the shiny spade was February 9th; he bore the turf away in a wheelbarrow of polished oak. The first hitch was at a point near Oakworth, when engineers and surveyors left instruments and plans some distance from where they were working. A cow tossed the levels and tripod away and began to eat the papers. That cow was owned by Messrs. Sugden, who were manufacturers at Oakworth, and a local newspaper abused the cow for holding up the work, adding that "the Haworthites had been planning for this railway for 15 years and this contretemps must be very disappointing."

There was nothing light-hearted about the way the builders laid metals in the Worth Valley. It was important to the prosperity of the district that a rail link should be established and on sod-cutting day the bells of Haworth Church were rung. Brontë's successor at the parsonage, the Rev. John Wade, prayed for the success of the undertaking at a Haworth repast. Later, daft stories began to circulate, and William Wright (Bill o'th' Hoylus End) wrote *T' History o't 'Awcrth Railway fro th' end, wi' an ackaant o'th' oppnkin' suremun,* which has been reprinted by the Keighley and Worth Valley Railway Preservation Society and is available at Haworth Station. The hungry cow gave the lines its first touch of ridicule, and soon people were telling of the Haworth man who showed his enthusiasm for the building of the line by making a barrow in the cellar of his house. When he had driven in the last nail he found it too big to be taken from the house! Another man, hopeful of being appointed porter, practised shutting carriage doors by slamming the oven door at home, shouting "All out for 'Owarth". He caught the cat's tail with one crisp door slam, and had a Manx cat to bear witness to his ability.

Money which would have been well spent on the railway was siphoned off by many legal wrangles. The weather could be very unkind, and in November, 1866, a cloudburst on the hills above Oxenhope flooded sections of the track, carrying away sleepers, rails and ballast. Four months went by before the damage had been made good.

The locomotive of the first train baulked at the first gradient, just outside Keighley Station. The track had been made greasy by a shower of rain. Spectators crowded round the train and invited the notables who were riding inside it to get out and push! Eventually the train was backed into Keighley Station and the journey re-started with a rush that took the train beyond the gradient without difficulty.

There was slow progress beyond Oakworth with another testing incline. The locomotive did not pass the test, even though men scattered ashes on the track. The train was divided and the first four carriages were taken forward to Haworth. Then the engine returned to complete its task. Haworth was reached an hour and a half after the official time of arrival. As rain poured down people cheered it, and the local Volunteer Rifle Corps Band led the distinguished guests to another large meal.

Worth Valley Railway was a local enterprise until 1881, and then Big Brother—the Midland Railway Company—took it over. Passenger services were withdrawn at the end of 1961, and that might have been the end of interest in the railway, with its push-and-pull trains, which in the latter days gave way to Diesel rail-cars. Some people had a quiet hope that the line would be revived, and that if British Railways could not be persuaded to re-open it some form of local enterprise (that type of enterprise which brought it into being) might be mustered.

Mr. G. R. Cryer, a technical college lecturer from Saltaire, called a public meeting at Keighley, and well over a hundred people attended it. The main decision was that a Keighley and Worth Valley Railway Preservation Society should be formed, and that it should begin negotiations with the Railways Board to see if a way could be found to keep the line open. Negotiations about the railway were protracted (that is nothing new in the railway history of the area), but in 1967 a formula was worked out which has enabled the trains to start puffing up the valley once again.

Haworth Railway Station is the headquarters of the Preservation Society and its operating company; here has been established a railway museum where visitors can inspect an array of old locomotives and rolling-stock. The Worth Valley line is being run in the best traditions of the old-time railways with trim stations and neat gardens. Steam trains are run along the whole length of the line during the summer season. Certain lighter-loaded trains consist of one or both of the small diesel rail buses. There is also a 500 horse-power diesel-electric locomotive. Many of the coaches have been restored to the liveries of the old-time railway companies.

The Brontës did not know the Worth Valley Railway. The fact that it lives on means that through it a large number of people will come to know the Brontës.

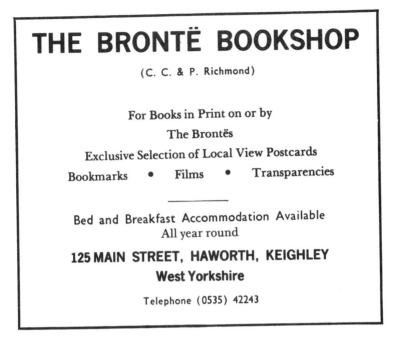

Wine and Dine in the olde worlde atmosphere of

the BLACK BULL HOTEL, Haworth.
famous for its Brontë connections

Full a-la-carte menu and extensive wine list
Specialised Sunday family lunch 12-2
Bar Snacks available at all times.

Fully Residential   Tel. Haworth 42249

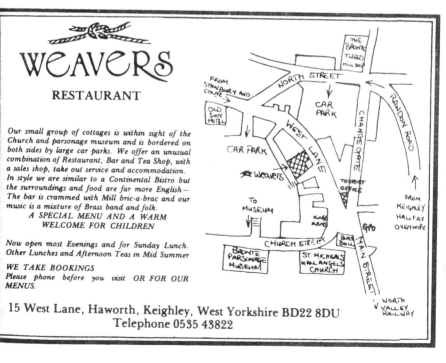

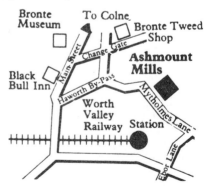